Nova Scotia

Can you smell it
coming down river?
It's winter

Text
Harry Bruce

Photographs
Gordon McGowan
Fred Joyce
Mervyn Kumar-Misir
Mary Primrose
Barbara Robertson
Alex Wilson
Janet Wilson
Tim Randall
Gordon R. Lay
John Thompson
Etta Parker
Robert H. Williams
Harold V. Green
Chic Harris

Design
René Demers
Craib Demers Associates
Limited

Line drawings
René Demers

Publisher
Anthony Hawke

Printed in Canada
by Heritage Press

Front cover
Sunset at Peggy's Cove

Back cover
The American Training Ship
"The Eagle" in Halifax Harbour

Library of Congress
Catalogue Card Number
74-84530

ISBN 0-88882-006-2

Hounslow Press
Toronto, Canada

Nova Scotia

Dinner is served.
Port Medway, South Shore

The facts are as dry as old bones but, like any
skeleton, they help define a physique. Nova
Scotia consists of about 21,000 square miles,
which makes it two thirds as big as Scotland,
and a little more than twice as big as Sicily.
Scotland and Sicily, however, each have more
than five times Nova Scotia's population
(about 800,000). Almost 80 percent of Nova
Scotia is forest land. Little more than
15 percent is farm land.

The rock beneath the forest's thin mattress, the
rock that rises to surround the farms in the river
valleys, the rock that bursts into the ceaseless
ocean wind all along the central spine of Nova
Scotia — and wherever the sea digs at the shore
— is among the oldest geological structures
known to Man. Hundreds of millions of years
have made it smooth and low by the standards
of such upstart rock formations as the Rocky
Mountains. Nowhere does it rise more than
1,800 feet. The burnishing and grinding of the
forces of time, however, have not made it
invariably hospitable to the people who choose
to live above it.

More facts: In places, Nova Scotia is 80 miles
wide, from salt water to salt water. Its total
length is 360 miles. But its shoreline — with

Nova Scotia

great fingers of sea stabbing for miles into the rock, the trees, the farmland — is longer than the breadth of the whole continent: 4,625 miles. More than 100 lighthouses and fog alarms help vessels find their way between the sea and the ports of Nova Scotia.

The neck of land that joins the province to New Brunswick is all that keeps Nova Scotia from being an island; and back in 1942, a writer named Dorothy Duncan had this to say about its island-like character:

"Except for the convenience to transportation of this seventeen-mile-wide isthmus, Nova Scotia is in every other sense an island, with all the self-conscious unity and distinction that every small inhabited bit of earth entirely surrounded by water seems to possess. Its outline is one of the most distinctive in the world; for no matter what it happens to be colored on a map it reminds almost everyone of a lobster. There its geographical simplicity ends, however; for no place is more difficult to fit into a single phrase".

The photographs that follow prove the difficulty; and at the same time, celebrate the beauty behind the facts.

Day breaks at Baccaro,
on the South Shore

Ornaments of Time

You may still find them here without much
trouble. Their time may be short. It may be as
short as the split second of a wave's curling into
foam; as the days of a wild rose's amazing
grace; as the weeks in which tiny, tough leaves
hurl a blaze of impossible red across the gray
face of shoreside stone that's hundreds of
millions of years old. Their life may be as short
as the secret decades in the rambling career of a
wilderness stream, the centuries in the rise and
fall of a single pine, or the millenia the sea
needs to shape rock to suit herself.

They are dying, flashing embellishments of old
and myriad cycles and, though they go, they
also return. The Mic Macs probably knew them
best. But the French knew them, too, and the
English, the New Englanders, the Scots, the
Irish, the Germans, the soldiers, sailors, traders,
the freed slaves, the farmers, fishermen, woods-
men and trappers. The wild bloom, the edge of
the forest, the barnacles and rockweed behind
the retreating tide, the salt-stunted spruce, the
calls of birds whose families are terribly ancient
. . . we share them with earlier men and women
who decided, for one brave reason or another,
to build their lives and their children's lives in
this hard country. We share these ornaments,
too, with the massive, free, unknown iceberg of
time before people ever set foot in the place
we call Nova Scotia.

For the moment,
the living is easy

Beyond the fields of summer,
the old forest waits.
Near Antigonish

Fireworks on stone.
Portuguese Cove

Death can be beautiful.
It supports life

Sometimes life finds a grip,
even on basalt. Brier Island

Cape Split says nothing,
and speaks for itself.
King's County

Barnacles and rockweed
hang on till
the tide's return

The marsh sleeps

Survivors.
Cape Breton Island

Watch out.
Something's coming.
Near Shelburne

The Weather

There's an old military meaning for the word "volant": it's "organized for rapid movement." And if there's one word to describe Nova Scotia weather, that's it. Volant. If you don't like our weather, Halifax people sometimes say, just wait an hour. In Nova Scotia, there's a trace of pride in the violent and dismal weather; you find fog-lovers, storm-lovers, even blizzard-lovers, and people who feel that, simply because they continue to live among the ferocious assaults of the weather, they must be especially tough. There's a trace of pride, too, in the perfect weather — in the peculiar, salty, pine-laden fragrance of a sweet summer morning, or the blazing calm of an October afternoon — but this pride feeds on an illusion.

Only a fool, Nova Scotians sometimes say, ever leaves Nova Scotia in the summertime. The truth is, Nova Scotia summers are not uniformly *anything* for much longer than it takes a hurricane to stampede its thunderous way through a reeling valley, or morning sunlight and an offshore wind to turn a gray zero of fog into a glittering sum of blue and gold all across the bay.

Sometimes, the snow falls here in June. Sometimes, a strange breeze of summer transforms a February afternoon into a wet, melting memory, a season with no name and a life you measure in minutes. Sometimes, the storms kill men at sea.

The widow-makers. They strike us still. Sometimes, the weather pummels an apple crop to death, wrecks fishing gear, tortures farm animals, hurls automobiles from the highways, forces good men to the dole and strangers to become friends, plunges whole towns into darkness and a thousand tourists into fits of depression. And sometimes, when the weather decides to treat Nova Scotia right, you would swear that this place was northern headquarters for the lotus-eaters.

Always, the weather has helped define the character of Nova Scotians and, among rural and seaside folk, it matters so much that for centuries they've had their own ways of out-guessing it. They've seen its future in the sounds of foghorns, train whistles, loons; in the way the leaves bend in the wind, potatoes cook in the pot, soot burns in the stove, smoke rises in the hills; in the look of the sun, moon, stars, northern lights, clouds and rainbows; in the order of arrival of wind, rain, and tide; in the behaviour of gulls, cranes, roosters, hens, earthworms, wasps, cattle, sheep, dogs, cats, spiders and locusts; in the feel of the corns on their feet, and a snowflake's weight. Often, their forecasts have been correct. Often, the forecasts of the government weather offices have been correct. Still, there has always come a time in which the weather has tragically or gloriously fooled just above everyone. That's because it is "volant."

14

Good morning!
Melville Cove, Halifax

Grey day,
Portuguese Cove

16

Fading day, fading year.
Shelburne County

There's a breeze blowin' up
at the mouth of the Margaree.
Cape Breton Island

Waiting it out.
Summerville, near Minas Basin

It's a fine, fair evening
but what about tomorrow?

A good day to stay ashore.
Southwest Margaree

21

Often, a sunset
mysteriously clears the sky

Moon and mist
compete for the night.
Digby Neck

23

What else is there to say?
It's springtime
in the Annapolis Valley.
Waterville

24

This morning, only the devout
will make their way to church.
St. Paul's Church,
the oldest building (1750) in Halifax

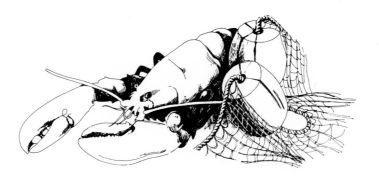

Fishing

The first western Europeans to visit Atlantic Canada after the Vikings were probably not the official explorers — with their flags and proclamations and dreams of a route to golden Cathay — but, rather, a few forever-unknown fishermen who may rarely have stopped work long enough to reflect on how fantastically brave they were. It was the fish that brought them here. The fish lured the men and, as the generations rolled on and became centuries the fish were the ceaseless inspiration for the building of God only knows how many thousands of vessels. Vessels to catch fish. Vessels to carry fish, and to bring home whatever the fish could buy in ports with strange names in strange countries. Vessels that took their graceful shape at hundreds of beaches and coves and harbours around Nova Scotia's massively intricate shoreline.

The fish then, if you follow the chain back far enough, were one reason for the growth of a trading economy, the maturing of master craftsmen in the ship-building business, the establishment of the timber industry, the survival of towns and, in remote farmhouses up and down the shore, the fact that in the depths of a cruel winter there would be something salty to eat with the boiled potatoes. The fish are the backbone of Nova Scotia's proud, sea-going tradition; and the tradition is no less real for being a cliché.

Nova Scotians who would never dream of risking their breakfasts aboard a Cape Islander in rough weather nevertheless display in their living rooms gorgeous photographs and paintings of storm-tossed schooners. And some, though they have comfortable city jobs, set and haul lobster traps in their spare time. They catch lobster because they want to, and because it is a Nova Scotian thing to do.

But what can you say about the men who still fish for their livelihood? What can you say that everyone does not already know? It is obvious they are brave. Most of them do get home, and live to fish again, but the odds are you would not enjoy going to sea to catch fish in March. It is obvious that, like all men who trust for their income on Nature's moods, they are gamblers. It is obvious they are independent to the point of being perverse. Why else would they stick to so grim a trade? It is obvious they are tough. Not tough in the pugnacious sense of the word, but tough like the glue oysters use to stick to a rock till they die. One thing that may not be obvious: other Nova Scotians are glad the fishermen are brave, gambling, stubborn, tough guys. Without them, Nova Scotia would not be Nova Scotia.

25

The sea is his business,
and maybe knowing it
keeps him young

Old salt,
with lobster pots

27

Nothing is so gracefully purposeful
as a well-kept dory.
Blue Rocks, near Lunenburg

How's she goin'?
Ingonish, Cape Breton Island

29   Neil's Harbour Lighthouse

End of a season.
Blue Rocks, near Lunenburg

31

With stone, wood, line —
and ancient skills —
anyone can make an anchor.
Isle Madame, Cape Breton Island

Tomorrow,
they have a job to do

33   Fish barrels

A good night's rest.
Neil's Harbour,
Cape Breton Island

Homestead, Digby Neck

Farming

Fishermen learned to become farmers. Farmers learned to become fishermen. Sometimes, fishermen and farmers learned to become miners and some, who grew tired of the mines, went back to survive as they could off the top of the land, the sea, or both. There are men in Nova Scotia who've followed half-a-dozen occupations at once. Since the time when every settler had to be a sufficiently skilled carpenter to build his own house (and maybe a boat, too), Nova Scotians have tried to be all things to all rural crafts. This has had little to do with native flightiness or a determination to be master of nothing. It was simply a matter of building survival out of available resources.

But just as some men spent their working lives exclusively in the fisheries, others spent theirs exclusively in farming. They were the ones who found themselves in valleys where the soil, by contrast with most of Nova Scotia, was miraculously rich and juicy. There, even the weather was hotter than the hard coasts could ever know. Wild old hills and a formidable wilderness separated these pockets of good farmland from one another, and from the fishing towns on the farther shores; and the farm communities grew up with legends, traditions, characters and habits of thrift of their own. They had an earthy insularity of attitude and, often, a certain suspicion of the jaded market city of Halifax.

You may see the decline of the family farm in the rotting shells of abandoned houses and barns in backroad fields around the province. But you may also see the rural family's old pride of place in the meticulously trim fields and gleaming wooden buildings of good farms that continue to survive the exodus of the young and the changing economic conditions of our own time. If the romance and sturdiness of Nova Scotia's seagoing tradition have performed any disservice at all, it is simply that they've overshadowed the culture and rich social history of all those Nova Scotians who stayed ashore to raise animals and reap harvests with roots.

Seeds of rain
in the Margaree Valley.
Cape Breton Island

37

Farm power in the old style,
Ross Farm, Lunenburg County

Hot day dying,
on a Nova Scotia farm

38

Near Margaree

Ripening season
in Cape Blomidon's lee

41

The hills wait.
The sounds of the farm are gone.
Margaree

The appearance of bliss
disguises the fact of sweat.
Near Truro

43

Autumn mountainscape,
from a pasture.
Cape North, Cape Breton Island

Downhill to a past with dignity.
Bras d'Or Lake,
Cape Breton Island

The agony in the forest,
Cape Breton Island

The French

France was finished as a giant power in North America more than two centuries ago. In Nova Scotia, there was no more dramatic symbol of her defeat than the British capture of Fortress Louisbourg on July 26, 1758. Louisbourg was both a fort and an entire walled town. It was one of the most massive, formidable and elaborate fortifications of its time. A brooding, magnificent and elegant expression of the power and style of 18th-century France, it is now a major tourist attraction.

Acadian French had lived in Nova Scotia for more than a century before the fall of Louisbourg and, for them, the saddest and most bitter consequence of the defeat of France was their forced expulsion by the British in the 1750s. Some ended up in New England, the Magdalen Islands, Louisiana, as far away as the West Indies but, following the formal peace of 1763, hundreds returned to Nova Scotia.

The plight of the expelled Acadians inspired Longfellow to write his sorrowful and romantic poem about "Evangeline" of Grand Pré. Her statue — and more authentic evidence of the French Acadian life and culture in the Annapolis Valley — may be found at Grand Pré National Historic Park. And the sturdiness of Acadian survival in Nova Scotia is still evident in family names, place names, and certain French-speaking shores and towns.

Evangeline's timeless sorrow,
and the little
church at Grand Pré

The construction of Louisbourg, begun in 1720, cost the royal French treasury thirty million livres, close to fifty million dollars in modern funds — an enormous sum for the times. The story is told that Louis XV remarked sardonically he expected some morning to open his windows at Versailles and see the towers of Louisbourg rising above the western horizon.

47

Under restoration,
mighty Louisbourg rises again

48

Louisbourg:
bell, clock tower, coat of arms

Chapel, Louisbourg.
The way it was more than
two centuries ago

High summer, Sandy Cove

Towns

A town may be a few fish huts and wooden houses hanging around a wharf; but long after men have quit using the wharf much, the town lingers on. A town may be a handful of shops and houses at a country crossroads; but long after the new shopping plaza on the paved highway has sucked away the crossroads trade, the town survives. Some towns defy apparent logic. It is easier to understand a city's existence. But what is it that keeps a particular town breathing in a particular place? Why don't the people just go away?

A town is a habit. It belongs to its people in a way no city ever belongs to anyone. A town is an extension of their living rooms and kitchens. The road through town, and its trees, are as familiar as an old bedspread. A town is a place in which children spend years getting to know other children, and then grow up, go away, and maybe never again set eyes on one another. Young people may itch to leave their town but, having left it, find it is with them forever. A few quit fighting the pull of the town, and come home to stay.

A town is a place where a few hundred people go to four churches. It is a place in which sea captains left their families. They returned, and brought rare things from places the neighbors would never see. It is a place where, after life-long struggles simply to survive the sea and wilderness, men and women found just enough time and just enough money for wooden gingerbread, the well-turned table-leg, stained glass, polished brass, lace and grace. A town is a memory. Sometimes, it looks as though it cannot survive another week but, decades from now, it will still be exactly where it is today. An older memory.

The spectators, Hunt's Cove

House of memories,
near Ship Harbour

53

Bedroom elegance,
W. D. Lawrence House,
Maitland

How the rich lived,
W. D. Lawrence House,
Maitland

54

55   Sunday afternoon,
Isle Madame

Tide's out, and so is school.
Digby

Gingerbread in the sky

Old and simple symmetry,
Port Royal

58

59

The dead end is at the sea,
Isle Madame

Gust in the wash,
beside St. John's Church,
Peggy's Cove

61

Closed till next Sunday,
Oakfield

62

Domestic dignity
in an old Loyalist town,
Ross Thompson House,
Shelburne

"Grey dawn, Halifax"

Halifax

Halifax, even more than most cities, is a packet of contradictions. Founded out of the fear of war, her own streets have rarely known anything but peace. The most violent wartime events Halifax has experienced were an accidental explosion when two ships collided in the harbour on December 6, 1917; and a sailors' riot on VE Day in 1945. (And VE Day, of course, was supposed to be the first day of peace in more than five years.) Founded to preserve peace, her economy has always thrived on war. She was a garrison town and, to some extent, still is. She was a seagoing town, a privateering town, a trading town, a busy, politicking, intrigue-ridden, profit-conscious, class-conscious, deeply British, parochial little port. And some insist she hasn't changed much.

Visitors to Halifax, particularly the involuntary visitors in the armed forces, have often detested it. In wartime, the air of homesickness was as heavy as the fog. Strangers often find Halifax both depressing and beautiful, both graceful and vulgar, both friendly and cold. But the people who were born in Halifax, and some who've moved there out of choice, are likely to insist it's God's gift to sensible living. It's small enough to be intimate but not so small it encourages nosiness. It's big enough to be culturally exciting but not so big it drowns you. It combines a certain amount of rich history with a certain amount of modern excitement. And, of course, though Haligonians may not remember it all the time, they know there's something special about spending the days and nights of their lives within earshot of a magnificent deepwater harbour. And under the unending influence of the sea.

64

Where steel meets the sea,
Halifax Harbour

Brunswick Street
from Citadel Hill

66

The year retreats,
Young Avenue

St. Paul's Cemetery,
closed for burials a century ago,
and St. Matthew's Church (1859)

In the famous Public Gardens
you can find a few moments of serenity
and share your lunch
with pigeons and ducks.

The Bluenose II is a replica of the Lunenburg fishing schooner that gained fame in the 1920's and 1930's by winning races against international competition. The replica was commissioned by a Halifax brewery and later presented to the province. The original Bluenose is commemorated on the Canadian ten cent piece.

Bluenose II

Fine art
from the great days of sail —
figurehead of H.M.S. Imaum
built at Bombay in 1826.
This Mona Lisa of the seas
now gazes placidly
at the Citadel's courtyard.

The Maritime Museum of Canada,
housed in the original Citadel

The old Town Clock (1803)
counts the minutes, and says
"Halifax, Halifax, Halifax"

Characteristic frame houses

74   St. Mary's Basilica (1829)
has the tallest
polished granite spire
in the world

Halifax skyline

LeHave River, Lunenburg County

Sundown

This book ends with sunsets. There is no
special reason for this. It's just that a sunset is
always a temporary good-bye.
It's just that, in Nova Scotia, the dying of the
day can be beautiful beyond explanation.

Cape John, Pictou County

Perfect end of a perfect day.
See you tomorrow

Mervyn Kumar-Misir has been active in photography from an early age. He is a teacher of Physics and Chemistry at the Dartmouth High School. He has gained numerous photography awards in International competitions and has twice received the Man-of-the-Year Trophy from the Photographic Guild of Nova Scotia for most points gained in club competitions.

Plate credits: 1, 14, 64, 78

Gordon R. Lay became interested in colour photography in 1956. Developing into a serious amateur, he achieved considerable success in world wide photographic salons. He is a member of The Photographic Guild of Nova Scotia and specializes in pictorial photography and photo-journalism.

Plate credits: 24, 43

Etta Parker is secretary to the Ombudsman for Nova Scotia. She is interested in many forms of photography, especially wildlife and nature. Etta combines her photography with canoe tripping, hiking, and cross country skiing. An active musician, Etta plays several instruments and enjoys reading. She has had numerous sports photographs published in Nova Scotia newspapers and in youth hostel brochures.

Plate credits: 72

Mary Primrose is the official photographer for the Biology Department of Dalhousie University in Halifax. She is an active member of the Photographic Guild of Nova Scotia and a member of N.A.P.A. She has had her work published in various scientific journals, but considers Portraiture as one of her chief interests in photography.

Plate credits: 9, 26, 65, 66, 68

Fred Joyce, was born in Ontario but has lived in Nova Scotia for the past 30 years. He is retired from the Canadian Armed Forces where he served as a Medical Laboratory Technologist and Medical Photographer. He has been active in photography from an early age and especially enjoys nature work. Fred is an active member of The Photographic Guild of Nova Scotia in club programming, and recently served as chairman of three seminars on photography in Halifax sponsored by the National Association for Photographic Art Inc. He also serves as the Atlantic Zone Director for N.A.P.A.

Plate credits: 4, 7, 11, 25, 61, back cover

Gordon McGowan developed an interest in photography in his native England. Originally this interest was in the monochrome medium, but since coming to Canada in 1957 he has become completely involved with colour photography. He has won numerous awards in both Regional and International competitions. His Travelogue Slide Shows, and his original colour prints of land and seascapes have received wide popular acclaim. Gordon works with CBC radio in Halifax.

Plate credits: Front cover, 2, 15, 18, 27, 34, 70, 71, 74, 76

Tim Randall came to Canada from England as a youth and settled in Halifax in 1929. He got involved in photography as a hobby in the early 40's and became a charter member of the Colour Photographic Guild of the Maritimes. He has been a member of the Photographic Society of America for 21 years and N.A.P.A. for 4 years and serves as a travel aid for both. Tim specializes in making travel sets and photo essays from his slide collection and has a wide knowledge of the photographic possibilities in Nova Scotia.

Plate credits: 37, 38, 40

Barbara Robertson, a member of The Photographic Guild of Nova Scotia, works as a writer at the Nova Scotia Museum. She likes to search out and photograph examples which illustrate a theme or current topic of interest, such as barn architecture, fishing boats and fishing gear, decorative ironwork, and unusual signs.

In 1974, Barbara was awarded a grant under the Explorations Program of The Canada Council. The award was given to assist her in making a written and photographic record of sawmills in Nova Scotia.

Plate credits: 13, 16, 21, 23, 63

John Thompson has been involved in photography for 20 years. He received his initial training with the Royal Canadian Navy in 1952 and served 4 years as a Naval Photographer. In 1957, he left the field of photography for about 10 years. Deciding to approach picture making from a non-commercial level for a while, he found that he enjoyed photography more than he used to and now takes almost all his photographs for his own satisfaction.

Plate credits: 56, 75

Alex Wilson is a native Nova Scotian and is a technologist with the Department of Biology at Dalhousie University in Halifax. He has been active in a wide range of photographic areas, including Nature, Land and Seascapes, Contemporary, Macro and Micro photography. He is a member of The National Association for Photographic Art Inc., and is Vice-President of the Photographic Guild of Nova Scotia.

Plate credits: 28, 47, 49, 53, 54, 62

Janet Wilson is a native Nova Scotian and is an instructor in Molecular Biology at Dalhousie University in Halifax. A relative new comer to the serious pursuit of photography, Janet has been working in the 35 mm format for just over a year. She is a member of The Photographic Guild of Nova Scotia.

Plate credits: 77

Harry Bruce is a Toronto-born freelance writer who decided in 1971 to settle with his wife, three children (and a black cat) in Nova Scotia. The motives for his decision were complex. They involved Bruce family roots in Nova Scotia that extend to the time when Napoleon was young. They involved a certain weariness with big-city life, an irrational conviction that the best sailing is salt-water sailing, childhood memories of summers "down home", a hunch about the sea. They involved, too, the facts that the photographs in this book prove: the simple facts of Nova Scotia's beauty. Beauty, he says, lies in the eye of every determined beholder of Nova Scotia. He does not think it likely he'll ever leave Nova Scotia for long.

Acclaimed by many critics as the best essayist in Canada, Harry Bruce is the author of "The Short Happy Walks of Max MacPherson" and countless articles which have appeared in newspapers across the country and in Maclean's, Canadian Magazine, Weekend, Readers Digest, Saturday Night and other magazines.

Bob Williams, AFIAP, a native of Halifax was a professional cinematographer for the Canadian Broadcasting Corporation for 16 years. He was promoted to Manager of Film Operations in Halifax in 1970. He has been active in the Photographic Society of America for the past 17 years and is presently rated in PSA as a 5 star exhibitor. Bob is a member of the Photographic Guild of Nova Scotia, and was recently honoured by the International Federation of Photographic Art as an associate for his work in photography and exhibition record in international salons.

Plate credits: 69

Harold (Hal) Green, APSA, a research microscopist, was born in Montreal. As a photojournalist, he is known for his many illustrated articles and book illustrations published in a score of countries. He was one of the photographers for the book Montréal, published by Hounslow Press in 1974.

Plate credits: 3, 8, 10, 12, 19, 22, 29, 32, 33, 35, 41, 46, 48, 50, 55, 57, 58, 59

Chic Harris has made photography his career since his retirement as a research chemist in 1966. His photographs have appeared in many books and periodicals, including "Montréal" published by Hounslow Press in 1974.

Plate credits: 5, 6, 17, 20, 30, 31, 36, 39, 42, 44, 45, 51, 52, 60, 67, 73